D0370127

The
Handwritten
Bible

The Handwritten Bible
Volume I
First printing

ISBN 0-9746014-0-3
Copyright ©2003 by The Repossession Company, Inc.,
Youth Ministry
All rights reserved.
Printed in the United States of America

Printed by
Midstate Printing Corporation

For more information or for
additional copies, please contact:
Pure For God Ministries, inc.
3888 South Western Boulevard
Orchard Park, NY 14127
Phone: 716-312-8363
Email: info@PureForGod.org
www.PureForGod.org

We believe the Bible, both Old and
New Testaments, to be the perfect and
innerrant Word of God. We encourage you
to secure the complete Bible soon for a deep
and more complete insight into
God's truth.

Here's a look at everyday people's
private thoughts regarding pain and sadness,
joy and hope, life's emotions and experiences,
and how the Scriptures relate to them.

We have asked over 50 people from all over
the world to journal their most intimate
thoughts and feelings on what the Bible
says about real life issues.

As you read, write down *your*
thoughts and opinions.

May you be blessed and find hope in
The Handwritten Bible.

Entries

Entries

"'Everything is MEANINGLESS,' says the Teacher, 'utterly meaningless! What do people get for all their hard work? Generations come and go, but nothing really changes.'"

✦✦ Ecclesiastes 1:2-5 ✦✦

Hey, My name is Dan. Having been at university for a year, I came home wondering exactly what King Solomon meant when he was talking in that verse. Throughout this entire past year I have just been amazed at the information and knowledge that people have. The cliché goes, "knowledge is power," but I couldn't help but think that knowledge is a bunch of compiled words that haughty men have studied for centuries. if I only learn what others have known before me, then what is my purpose? God answered that question later on in Ecclesiastes 2:25-26a: "For who can eat or enjoy anything apart from God? God gives wisdom, knowledge, and joy to those who please Him." I now realize that God gives wisdom and he also gives joy, which is what I want. I realized that through God, my wisdom gains purpose and He gives me joy, If I will choose to do what is pleasing to Him. Now, the following questions are just a few that I am asking you to take a look at and consider:

→ Do you feel that your life has meaning, even after you die?

→ How do you feel about human knowledge that is passed down in schools today?

→ Is knowledge empty at all?

→ Have you ever thought about how the knowledge of God would affect you?

・ ー ・ ー ・ ー ・

What do I think?

_____

_____

_____

_____

_____

_____

_____

_____

_____

_____

_____

_____

Psalm 40
v 1-3

I waited patiently for the Lord;
he turned to me + heard my cry.

He lifted me out of the slimy pit
   out of the mud + mire:

he set my feet on a rock
+ gave me a firm place to stand.

He put a new song in my mouth
   a hymn of praise to our Lord

~ Amen !

Clair's promise from Lord

Hi! My mum suffers from Multiple Sclerosis in a severe way + in many ways I no longer have a mum. For years I was so angry at God because He could've healed her + yet hasn't. I felt I was in a slimy pit as my family life just seemed to slide away from me + there was nothing I could do about it. But I covered this all up + just stayed angry at God. It was only when I began to trust God again + open myself up to Him that He started to lift me out of the pit. I still don't understand why all of this happened, but God has used me + has begun a new work in me. He has given me other family members through the Church + I've become a stronger person as I stand on God, my Rock.

LAMENTATIONS 3:21-25

Yet this I call to mind, and therefore I have hope: Because of God's great love, we are not consumed, for His compassions never fail. They are new every morning! Great is your faithfulness. I say to myself "the Lord is my portion; therefore I will wait for Him. The Lord is good to those whose hope is in Him, to the one who seeks Him".

VS 32 Though He brings grief, He will show compassion, so great is His unfailing love.

I present this scripture to you from the NIV version

My name is Janet Pfaff.

The Lord has used this Scripture in my life through the loss of my precious daughter. When I lost my child, comfort was at a premium and when I read these verses, I became comforted and hopeful. They minister peace, love, tenderness and compassion like only God can provide.

When you are faced with enormous trial and burdens, where do you turn for comfort?

My thoughts...

_____

_____

_____

_____

_____

_____

_____

FRANK

was impacted by
Psalm 68:5

"A father to the fatherless, a defender of widows, is God in his holy dwelling."

When I was 14 years old, my father died of a heart attack. He was my best friend, the person I trusted and loved. I felt incomplete without him. My mother also was badly hurt. This verse means so much to me because it lets me know that although my biological father is gone, my true father is with me.

Have you lost someone?

Are your parents divorced or unloving towards you?

Don't you just want to run into your fathers arms?

Run to God...

Isaiah 42:

v3. A bruised reed he will not break, and a smoldering wick he will not snuff out. In faithfulness he will bring forth justice.

v6b. I the LORD have called you in righteousness, I will take hold of your hand.

v9. See, the former things have taken place, and new things I declare; before they spring into being I announce them to you.

My name is Beth. I was 16 and miserable, scrambling for anything to kill the empty pain inside of me - dieting for "that body", cutting, hatred ...the occult.

It was July. I was unsure of what kind of life to pursue, confused about what to believe and how it affected the way I lived, and worrying about what would happen next.

I had a Bible in my hands—It fell open to this verse, and the words felt as if they had been written specifically to me.

It was as if God was speaking directly to me — "I see you, I know you, I love you. I know you're confused and hurting. Let me help you, I will be gentle. following me will not hurt or break you. You don't see yet what will happen, but I do... I have it all planned."

Those words were hope exactly when I needed them. I opened my heart to the love of God and began to trust him and he brought me to a place of wholeness in my life, my relationships, my future.

Even now, several years later, when doubt and fear tries to creep in, those words remain, strong

I THE LORD HAVE CALLED YOU IN RIGHTEOUSNESS. I WILL TAKE HOLD OF YOUR HAND.

"Not only so, but we rejoice in our sufferings because we know that suffering produces perseverance; perseverance, character; character, hope. And hope does not disappoint us because God has poured out His love into our hearts by the Holy Spirit, whom He has given us."

Romans 5:3-5

My name is Trevor Kaufman and this verse has recently helped me get through a horrible end to an engagement about 3 years ago. I can easily say that during that time I was going through some of the most intense suffering I could have ever imagined. When my fiancee broke up with me, I truly wanted God to take my life. However, instead of taking my life, He gave me this verse. How could I possibly rejoice in what happened to me? After focusing on this verse, I started to persevere, and climb out of the "hell" I was in. As I persevered, a new character started to develope within me that I hadn't experienced before. Through that character, I began to experience the hope of God in my life. With this hope I was able to see why God had put me through the pain I went through. I began to move on and was able to put the past behind me. In that time of healing God has put opportunities in front of me that I would have never been given had I still been with my Fiancee. Through the suffering, I was able to experience God's timing, provision, and most of all His love. That is something to rejoice about. And yes, I am in love with a new, beautiful and truly amazing women. My challenge is that you would look for the joy and new opportunities that lay ahead of your current sufferings, whatever they may be.

— Rejoice in your
                    sufferings —

Ps. 18:30 "As for God, his way is perfect; the word of the Lord is flawless. He is a shield for all who take refuge in Him."

Hi. I'm Sherri. In August of 2001 I read these words while sitting in Buffalo's Childrens Hospital next to my five year old daughter who had suddenly gone blind. She had, hours before endured a painful spinal tap procedure that was unsuccessful. I was angry. I was sad. I was alone. Nothing about the previous 24 hours had been perfect. The words stung and yet somehow they held before me a beautiful resolve. Rest and trust from all I don't understand. Psalm 18 goes on to say that God is giving us "hinds feet for high places."

$$\longrightarrow$$

That is — he was willing to give me everything I needed to make it through this steep and difficult climb.

I was angry at God and I was angry at myself for being angry at God — because it is truly pointless. He is my shield, my protection, my hope. To resist him in that hour of need would've been cursing the hand that fed me.

I didn't understand him, but I needed him! So I took my ugly, wounded, painful heart and collapsed on Him. Jesus says. "In this world, you will have trouble." — He wasn't kidding! "But take heart I have overcome the world." I am learning slowly — the only perfect place I can find is in Jesus... whether I understand it all or not. I am safe.

↯H

"Rejoice in the Lord always. I will say it again: Rejoice!" Let your gentleness be evident to all. The LORD is near. Do not be anxious about anything, but in everything, by prayer and petition, with thanksgiving, present your requests to God. And the peace of God, which transcends all understanding, will guard your hearts and minds in Christ Jesus."

"Finally, brothers, whatever is true, whatever is noble, whatever is right, whatever is pure, whatever is lovely, whatever is admirable - if anything is excellent or praiseworthy think about such things."
Philippians 4:4-8

My name is Dan. I am a 56-year-old retired automotive executive and follower of Christ who knows all about depression; that cold, lonely, dark place where nothing is enjoyable, where restful sleep eludes you, and you have regular thoughts about how the world would be better off without you.

Thanks to a loving wife who gently guided me to medical help, the depression was diagnosed and chemically treated.

15

At this point I found this Verse and my Life began to heal. Using Verses six and seven as a guide, I began telling God about ALL my negative thoughts and emotions and how much I missed the joy in my Life. I held nothing back and for the first time in years I had Peace. I also followed verse eight's admonition to think about (visualize) all the things it described. As I did, I felt better about myself and joy returned. Further, I now have the assurance of verse Seven that JESUS CHRIST now guards my heart and mind.

"Rejoice in the LORD always. I WILL SAY IT Again: Rejoice!"

Personal reflections...

"For my thoughts are not your thoughts, neither are your ways my ways, declares the Lord As the heavens; higher than the earth, so are my ways higher than your ways.

So is my word that goes out of my mouth; It will Not return empty, but it will accomplish what I desire, and acheive the purpose for which I sent it."

Isaiah 55:8,9,11

Hi I'm Katie. Have you ever gone through something in life where you find yourself asking.. "**WHY?**"

Many times things happen that we just don't understand. In the past four years my family and I have moved three times, all for various reasons that brought difficult changes and transitions in my life. Confused and frusterated, I began to ask myself **WHY** God did this to my family and what the ending result of it would be. Then, through time, I realized it wasn't His job to be my fortune teller. I don't need to know the future, and now I don't even want to know because me - the human - would probably mess it up anyways.

What are you asking **WHY** about?

MY NAME IS TERRI. "I PRAY ALSO THAT THE EYES OF YOUR HEART MAY BE ENLIGHTENED IN ORDER THAT YOU MAY KNOW THE <u>HOPE</u> TO WHICH HE HAS CALLED YOU, THE <u>RICHES</u> OF HIS GLORIOUS INHERITANCE IN THE SAINTS, AND HIS INCOMPARABLY GREAT <u>POWER</u> FOR US WHO BELIEVE." (EZEKIEL 18:31).

I WAS STRUGGLING PROFESSIONALLY, FINANCIALLY, SPIRITUALLY, AND EMOTIONALLY AFTER THE PAIN OF AN UGLY DIVORCE. I HAD 2 YOUNG CHILDREN TO RAISE AND THE FANTASY THAT I COULD DO IT ON MY OWN.

I HAD HEARD THAT A PERSON IS AS GOOD AS THE BOOKS HE READS, THE TAPES HE LISTENS TO, AND THE PEOPLE HE ASSOCIATES WITH. I STARTED READING THE BIBLE. AND I LEARNED THERE WAS <u>HOPE</u> FOR ME. HOPE FOR A FUTURE. GOD PROVED THAT TO ME. AS I MADE READING THE BIBLE PART OF MY DAILY LIFE, OVER TIME HE BLESSED ME WITH A PROMOTION AT WORK THAT LED TO LESSENED FINANCIAL BURDENS THAT ALLOWED MY SELF-ESTEEM TO RETURN. IT HAS BEEN YEARS SINCE I STARTED EXPERIENCING THE AWESOME POWER OF BELIEVING IN GOD'S PLAN FOR ME. I AM REMARRIED, HAVE 2 MORE BEAUTIFUL CHILDREN, AND CONTINUE TO EXPERIENCE GOD'S BLESSINGS DAILY!

HAVE YOU READ YOUR BOOK TODAY?

My thoughts...

MATTHEW 5:6

"Blessed are those who thirst for righteousness for they will be filled"

_____ my name is

JAKE

I'm sure I speak for everyone when I say I hate feeling like trash. I hate feeling like there is more out there than what I knew or have, No matter what I did to take that feeling away it was always temporary. As fast as I felt better I felt like trash again, when I read this verse it showed me that the only Thing I needed was God. I know now that if I read the Bible and talk to God and tell him my problems I feel complete. If you know how I feel; read the Bible. read the section called John. I know God wont let you down. Sex, drugs, and other quick fixes are an empty answer and will leave you feeling just as bad again. ONLY God fills you completely.

All for God or nothing at all.

What I think...

"For the poor, every day

brings trouble;

for the happy heart,

life is a continual

feast."

Proverbs 15 v15

hey, my name is emily.
I find this versechallenges
me alot.

It is saying
that for people who look
at the bad side of life
or what goes wrong for
them will usually be
quite depressed! But if
you (choose) to see the
best in a situation,then
it makes life a lot more
enjoyable. Its important to
make the right decision
What kind of person
are you? (smile!)

My feelings about this...

_____

_____

_____

_____

_____

_____

"Be patient with each person, attentive to individual needs. Be careful that when you get on each others nerves so that you don't snap at each other. Look for the best in each other, and always do your best to bring it out.

Be cheerful no matter what; Pray all the time; THANK GOD NO MATTER WHAT HAPPENS.

This is the way God wants you who belong to Christ Jesus to live.

— 1 Thessalonians 5: 15-18 —

Hey. I'm *Andrea. When I first read this, I was Miserable

No matter how hard I tried to look happy, I couldn't fake it. I was constantly putting my friends down and being mean to my family. I couldn't understand why they backed away from me when I needed them the most. I was rude and bitter and thought I deserved better than the circumstances I was facing — I was alone and unhappy. When I finally realized how truly miserable I was, I did A LOT of apologizing, and I read this verse 15 times over. No matter what the circumstances are, God is not to blame. If I had taken my eyes off myself, maybe I would've noticed Him.

He never stopped loving me.

"HE WILL COVER YOU WITH HIS FEATHERS; UNDER HIS WINGS YOU WILL FIND REFUGE; HIS FAITHFULNESS WILL BE YOUR SHIELD... YOU WILL NOT FEAR

THE TERROR OF NIGHT!"

I'm BRAD! THESE TWO VERSES, PSALMS 91:4-5 HELPED ME FACE & OVERCOME A TERROR THAT STRUCK ME AT 2:00 A.M.

I WAS BATTLING VERTIGO (DIZZINESS). FOR ABOUT THREE MONTHS. ONE NIGHT I WOKE UP TERRIFIED, SWEATING WITH MY HEART RACING. IT WAS PITCH BLACK IN MY ROOM and BECAUSE OF MY DIZZINESS, I WAS DISORIENTED AND FELT LIKE I WAS FALLING HELPLESSLY INTO AN ENDLESS BLACK HOLE.

I Thought I HAD DIED!
I thought I was facing Eternity
I thought "Oh No . Darkness forever"

I CRIED OUT "GOD PLEASE Help ME!" AT THAT MOMENT I LOOKED AND SAW THE LIGHT OF MY ALARM CLOCK... I began to think "HEY.. THERE AREN'T ANY ALARM CLOCKS IN ETERNITY". THE WORDS OF THIS PSALM BEGAN TO COMFORT ME. I QUIETED DOWN, rested AND THE TERROR slowly faded AWAY.

⭑ Is <u>NIGHTTIME</u> A <u>TERROR TIME</u> for you?
BAD DREAMS - NIGHTMARES
FEAR - LONELINESS - ANXIETY!

Just cry out "Help ME Jesus" Call out "Father comfort me". He <u>WILL</u> HEAR you, He WILL ANSWER. He IS <u>ABLE</u> TO DISPENSE the terrors of To NIGHT.

<u>Earlier</u> in Ps 91:1 it says - "He/she WHO DWELLS IN THE SHELTER OF THE MOST HIGH (God), <u>WILL</u> rest in THE SHADOW OF THE ALMIGHTY".

Just repeat these words over; over Again when Night Terrors come — God <u>WILL</u> respond. I'M LIVIN' PROOF!!!

Romans 8:38-39

"For I am convinced that neither death nor life, neither angels nor demons, neither the present nor the future, nor any powers, neither height nor depth, nor anything else in all creation, will be able to seperate us from the love of God that is in Christ Jesus our Lord."

In The Divine Conquest by A.W Tozer, the author makes the following statement about God:

"We talk of Him much + loudly but in our hearts we wonder if he's really there."

My name is Carli and for most of my life that statement described my relationship with God better than the trust shown in Romans 8:38,39. I knew there was a God and that I needed to believe in Him, but I felt way too much lonliness + confusion to believe he cared about me + loved me. I wondered why I didn't "feel" anything when I prayed or why I didn't hear anything. I came to believe that a relationship with God could only be one way, me doing all the talking with no response from God. So I would pray and say I believed but I knew he wouldn't answer me.

If you are feeling or thinking that way let me tell you that it's all wrong. God loves us and wants to talk to us, He wants to <u>show</u> us His love.

When I was sixteen I was praying one night that God would use me and right there he spoke to me. For the first time I knew He loved me + that he hadn't been ignoring me.

Hebrews 13:5 from <u>The Message</u>, God says to us, "I'll never let you down, never walk off and leave you." Again from <u>The Message</u>, John 10:10, Jesus says, "I came so they (meaning you + I) can have real + eternal life, more and better life than they ever dreamed of."

Pray and ask God to give you a better life than you ever dreamed of, the one he has planned for you. The one that shows how much he loves you and nothing can separate you from that love!

Hello! I'm Sarah — and I want to share a verse with you that changed the way I view Jesus.

"Jesus wept."
John 11:35

Its the shortest verse in the Bible, but it speaks volumes. These two words tell an amazing story. "Jesus" is the most powerful name in the universe. When Jesus' name is mentioned, some get angry and others feel joy. At this name, knees bow and demons flee. Jesus had the power to split time in half and our calendar and holidays are based on His birth, death and resurrection. Jesus was born with all the power of the universe at His fingertips. But the second word in the verse seems strange. It doesn't seem like it describes the divine King Jesus is. To two who weep is to feel pain, to understand suffering and grief. To weep is to feel human. So why did Jesus, ruler of the universe, choose the life of a poor and

31

homeless human? why did He subject Himself to pain and suffering? Because when He saw me and knew that I would sin and go to hell, Jesus wept. You see, all He ever wanted was to spend eternity in heaven with His precious creation, me! And so He lowered Himself from the comforts of heaven, taking on the restraints of humanity, and paying the ultimate price on the cross. This He did for _you_ too. He chose to die for you. Choose to live for Him.

My thoughts...

_____

_____

_____

_____

_____

_____

_____

_____

_____

The Lord is my light and my
salvation, whom shall I fear?
The Lord is the stronghold of my
life of whom shall I be afraid?

Psalm 27:1

For God did not give us a spirit
of fear, but a spirit of power,
of love and self-discipline.

2 Timothy 1:7

Hi! My name is Joelle and I am
15 years old. Fear is something
I deal with on a daily basis,
whether it is just walking into
a store and asking a question
or getting up in front of a
group to speak. But there is
a song made out of the
verses above and whenever
I start to feel a little nudge

of fear the song just pops into my head. I feel that God puts the song in my head to push me to do whatever I am afraid to doo. Singing this song helps me to get over my fear of going to meet a new person or introducing myself to a group. I think to myself God _is_ there and He _is_ in charge so what am I afraid of?

When I think that, I am able to go up and meet that new person. God calms my heart and helps me to think clearly.

What can you do to stop letting fear control your life?

How can God help?

"Come to Me, all you who labor
and are heavy laden, and I will
give you rest."

This was spoken by Jesus Christ in the
book of Matthew Chapter 11:28.
My name is Peter. I've worked in Florida and
been in Hong Kong and North Carolina.
We can be heavy laden with
bricks on our shoulders, or we can
be laden with heavy emotions or
heavy responsibility. This quotation
isn't specific. It says Jesus will
give us rest. Rest is so nice.

As each of my children have hit
their teen years I have been laden
with the need to teach them to live
responsibly, and to let them learn
on their own. This is a hard lesson for

me. I struggle with it as they learn and as they fail once or twice. When I get over laden I need rest. Deep rest that doesn't come at night in bed, but that comes in my emotions. Jesus loves my children more than I do. He can take care of them and guide them. I can rest because He cares.

What do I think about this?

_____

_____

_____

_____

_____

_____

_____

_____

_____

36

II Timothy 1:7

For God hath not given us the spirit of fear; but of power, and of love; and of sound mind.

Hi, I'm Debbie Yager. In my life I have found "fear" to rear its ugly face in many forms. I've always struggled with worthiness. In areas of my life where I do not feel worthy, I develop fears of acceptance. And, as our minds tend to do, the fear grows... and blows everything out of proportion. When I found II Timothy 1:7, it seared through my heart. I memorized it, and began to quote it in my head every time I became anxious. God began to cover me with peace and comfort. I found that reaching for God and His Words not only took the focus off my fears, but

clearly opened my eyes....
to who holds the key to my
strength.

The Bible claims to be sharper
than a two edged sword. I in
desperation boldly used it as
such ... and God sliced that
fear to the stem. I even today
am in "awe" of this way that
God blessed me. I do not take
this lightly though, and fully
realize that as a garden needs
constant tending ... so does
this weakness in my life. I
must constantly check myself.
And these days when fears and
struggles creep into my life,
I get that Holy Biblical sword
... and start weed wacking!

I urge you to boldly use God's
Word, with faith and confidence.
You too will find your life ...
and your garden ... with less
weeds ... and much greater
beauty.

Dave here. Here's a short story from my life and how it really changed the way I think of Heaven.

Revelation 21:3+4

"Behold, the tabernacle of God is with men, and He will dwell with them, and they shall be His people. God Himself will be with them, and be their God. And God will wipe away every tear from their eyes; there will be no more death, nor sorrow, nor crying. There shall be no more pain, for the former things have passed away."

On January 26, 1998 a very close friend came to our house to pray with my mom. Mom had a brain tumor and she was dying. As my friend began to pray I closed my eyes. She started talking to my mom about a river mentioned in Isaiah 66:12. As she prayed I saw from a distance a woman stepping out of a River onto dry land. As she stood up, she reached and took the hand of someone who seemed to be waiting there for her. When their hands met I was overcome with emotion and cried. She had taken the hand of Jesus! He was the one waiting for her; now I knew she would be ok and it was ok to let her go. She would soon feel a love so deep that I had cried just seeing it from a distance. three days later she stepped out of the river that we are living in right now. He took her hand and welcomed her into eternity because she had asked Him to be in her life. The Bible says that if you ask He'll come into your life too. Heaven is going to be so sweet!

PROVERBS 17 v 17:

"
"A friend loves at all times,
but a brother is born for
adversity."

I often find myself failing
and being failed as a friend.
You need to hear me clearly
on this! It doesn't matter how
much, I, or my friends try, we
will always let each other down.
I don't know if you've ever been
betrayed by one of your best
friends or if you've been let
down by someone so close to
you that you feel like life
isn't worth really trying with

anymore. I've felt like this so much and this verse is something I hold dear to me. When I think about Jesus I know that I have a friend who loves me at all times. I see Judas betray him in the gospels, his closest friends deny they know him when he needs them most and he responds by loving them and giving them value. I try to be a friend who loves at all times and I really want to be just that. But when everything around me fails, I know Jesus has been in that situation as well and he loves me at all times. He loves you too, no matter who you are... and for all time!!!

2 Corinthians 5:6-9 ✝

"Now we look forward with confidence to our heavenly bodies, realizing that every moment we spend in these earthly bodies is time spent away from our eternal home in heaven with Jesus. We know these things are true by believing, not by seeing. And we are not afraid, but are quite content to die, for then we will be at home with the Lord. So our aim is to please Him always in everything we do, whether we are here in this body or away from this body and with Him in heaven."

Hi I'm april!

It was a usual, uneventful Monday, May 24, 1999 to be exact ... until I got a horrifying call that evening from my dad, "April, get to the hospital! Your sister Amy has been in a very bad car accident!"

That day would change our lives forever - Amy died instantly in the crash, only 22 years old, just nine days after her college graduation. The questions, the pain, the sudden loss was more than I could take. She was not just my sister, but my friend. We had grown <u>so</u> <u>close</u> over the years.

In my deep despair I turned to God for help, many times just to get me through another day without Amy. As I read 2 Corinthians 5, my perspective on "life" began to shift. Amy wasn't dead, she was more ALIVE now than ever! She had reached her <u>eternal</u> home - face to face with her Lord Jesus.

Missing Amy never stops, but I "<u>LOOK</u> <u>FORWARD</u> <u>WITH</u> <u>CONFIDENCE</u>" that we <u>WILL</u> be together again - FOREVER!

♡ I love you, Amy-Pie ♡ xoxoxo

Hebrews 4:12-13

"For whatever God says
to us is full of living power:
it is sharper than the sharpest
dagger, cutting swift and
deep into our innermost
thoughts and desires with
all their parts, exposing us
for what we really are.

He knows about everyone,
everywhere. Everything about
us is bare and wide open
to the all seeing eyes of our
living God; nothing can be
hidden from him to whom
we must explain all that
we have done."

Wow! The power and
precision of God's word! It
gets right down to the center
of who I am because nothing
is hidden from God. It isn't
just the big things he
notices, but the small, petty
things as well. Why do I
sometimes live as if the

small things I do that are
bad don't count?

God cares so much about
me and about you that he
is concerned about everything
in our lives. We can't fool
him about who we are
because he knows us —
even better than we know
ourselves, and loves us
anyway!

The truth that God knows
EVERYTHING about me has
made a difference to me in
this past year. I want to know
what will please him and
what I should stay away
from, so I have been reading
my Bible every day. I want
to know God better, so I
read what he has to say to
me.

Isn't it great that a wife,
mother and grandmother in her
mid 50's can still learn more
about God?

JoEllen

"... Your sins have been your downfall! Take words with you and return to the Lord saying to Him " Forgive us all our sins and recieve us graciously, that we may offer the fruit of our lips... for in you the fatherless find compassion.'"

Hosea 14:1-3

My name is Nancy

So many times in life we defer the blessing God has been waiting to give us. Our sin and letting it build up inside of us prevents us from recieving the fullness and riches He wants to bless us with.

When I choose my own will, it always leads to sin. When I then try to do what God wants, with unrepentence in my heart, I will continue to fall. A vicious cycle of failure, guilt and sinning begins to take hold of my life.

God wants to set you and I free. He wants to change that vicious cycle into a victorious one, consisting of blessing, and fullness and wholeness in Him. Only when we let everything go and ask Him for forgivness will we completely recieve all the amazing things He has instore for us.

yes, we will fail and we will sin; But if we then choose to stay close to God at those times by repenting and accepting forgivness in Him, we will be continually renewed.

-¦- Lay down your sins to recieve His full blessing!! -¦-

" Salvation is found in no one else, for there is no other name under heaven given to men by which we must be saved."

Hey, my name is Robin. This is found in the Bible, the book of Acts, Chapter 4 and verse 12.

This verse might be tough to understand, maybe even agree with, but keep reading & let me explain it to you.

My life is different now that I've come to understand this verse, Jesus' words.

Of all the names today, one name is more powerful than any other, the name is Jesus. This name rescues lost, lonely people, heals the sick, changes our lives secures our eternity.

Now in this world, so many things call out to us to be our Savior. Things like relationships, sex, a good job, popularity, the newest drug, money, etc.

At one time in my life I was ignorant that God had a great plan for my life. I was enjoying a smorgasbord of "so-called" saviors. Then one day I picked the right Savior, Jesus. I examined Jesus up against the other saviors + Jesus was + still is the best.

This Savior, Jesus, can help you with all aspects of your life, your pain, your disappointments and insecurities. He is able to forgive all your mess ups and sins. You will never have a true peace + rest inside until you choose the right Savior. Will you choose Jesus?

> But u R a chosen People, a royal priesthood, a holy nation, a People belonging 2 God, That u may declare the Praises of him who called u out of darkness into his wonderful light
>
> 1 Peter 2:9

Hi, I'm **Steph!** For years and years, I struggled with feeling accepted. I had an alcoholic father and when I was 19, my mother died. After she died, I moved around to a lot of different houses and never felt accepted.

Someone showed me 1 Peter 2:9 and prayed with me! I just want you to know that _Jesus Christ_ _accepts_ and _loves_ us, no matter what we've been

51

through! He leads us out of darkness and into light!! His purpose for us all is to be <u>loved</u> and <u>accepted</u>!

My impressions...

S2

Hi, my name is Kathy! The verse I want to share with you is 2 Peter 1:3 - His divine power has given us everything we need for life and godliness through our knowledge of him who called us by his own glory and goodness,

I love this verse! It sums up for us just how much God loves us. Have you ever thought about being a Christian and then said, "No that would be too hard."

This verse tells us that God not only wants us to be a Christian but He gives us the power that we need to live a Godly life. In fact, no one can really live a Godly life without Christ. The more that we know Him, the more we realize just how much

He gives us.
I can't imagine life without Christ. I pray that you will take the time to get to know Him. You see, life without Christ is really no life at all.

Personal reflections...

_____
_____
_____
_____
_____
_____
_____
_____
_____
_____
_____
_____
_____
_____
_____
_____
_____
_____
_____
_____

54

John 15: 10-11

If you obey my commands, you will remain in my love, just as I have obeyed my fathers commands and remain in his love. I have told you this so that my joy may be in you and that your joy may be complete.

What's up? My Name is Ben, Did you Know that Christ wants us to love and obey Him just as he loved & obeyed his father? Obedience Keeps us connected to him.

ss

True joy can only be found in obeying God. Obedience brings Joy, and God's Joy is complete. When we obey God we bring him joy. Have you personally experienced the joy that Christ Brings, What changes can you make In your life that will make Christ Happy?

Notes...

_____

_____

_____

_____

_____

_____

_____

_____

_____

_____

_____

_____

_____

_____

_____

_____

✳ PSALM 23 ✳

The LORD is my shepherd,
I shall not be in want. He makes
me lie down in green pastures,
he leads me beside quiet waters,
he restores my soul. He guides
me in paths of righteousness for
his name's sake. Even though
I walk through the valley of the
shadow of death, I will fear no
evil, for you are with me, your
rod and your staff they comfort me
You prepare a table before me
in the presence of my enemies. You
anoint my head with oil, my cup
overflows. Surely goodness and love
will follow me all the days of my
life, and I will dwell in the house
of the Lord for ever.

✳ Amen ✳

Hello ☺! My name is Feruza.
I just wanted to share with
you how God was looking
after me when I was away
from home.

I spent 2 years in UK, doing the course and working in school, sharing the good news. It was my first time away from home and I was really scared to go. But this psalm reminded me that God is good! He cares for us, looks after us. Even when we go through hard times, he is alway there right besides us, You know why? Because He loves us!

xxx

What I think...

58

Hello — I am Jackie — wife, mother, professional consultant and in ministry as God leads.

Colossians 3:2 says "Set your affections on things above."

Now in mid-life, I am accepting God's perspective that "setting my affections on things above" means living simply here below. Through pain of divorce, abortion, wanting control and busyness, God has taught me that today, here and now, in the everyday routines of life, I am to stay close to Him and those around me. You know — short, honest prayers and less fault finding

I also now have a long term perspective on life, asking more regularly, "How important is this?" Fewer things are now important enough to break my peace with God or with those He has placed in my world. There is less desire to withhold my affection, to hold on to prolonged anger, resentment, or self pity.

Lord Jesus, help me to love you and others with pure and simple affection.

What I think...

_____
_____
_____
_____

60

Trust in the Lord with all your heart, and lean not on your own understanding, In all Your ways acknowledge Him, and He will direct your Paths. Proverbs 3:5

God is completely TRustworthy, but at one time I wasn't so sure. I didn't easily tRust for I felt let down by people all my growing up years. Until three years ago when I underwent open ♡ surgery.

I'm Sue, a wife and mom of 2 beautiful children and finding I need to trust God with my whole life. Needless to say I prayed alot and asked others to pray. Here's what God did:

① His timing was perfect. for my surgery, for that very morning of my surgery I Started having problems that only the surgery could correct. God's plan was Right on schedule.

② I had no pain.

③ The nurses were caring and helpful.

④ My roommate was a gem.

God took care of all my fears and my life too!

He showed me He is completely trustworthy! He means it not just for me — But you too!

Won't you Trust Him today?

God will direct your path too — If you let Him!

Jeremiah 29:11

"For I know the plans I have for you," declares the Lord, "plans to prosper you and not to harm you, plans to give you hope and a ~~future~~."

My name is Aimee and I am 29 years old. Five years ago my daughter Katie was diagnosed with a heart condition called Long QT syndrome. There is no cure for this genetic condition, and it could cause sudden death. Sadly, my brother Chad died from this when he was 13 years old, while swimming. Losing my brother was very painful and difficult to try to understand. As if that couldn't be enough, my daughter's life was now in danger.

After Katie was diagnosed my whole world changed! Worry filled my life, and the stress and anxiety became overwhelming. The fear of losing my daughter now consumed my every thought. I lost my joy and my happiness. Some days when I woke up, I didn't even want to get out of bed.

I couldn't handle one more heart break!

One day while Katie was playing outside, I lost sight of her. In a panic, I ran around the house, my heart pounding, terrified I would find her on the ground! But there she was, smiling and laughing, chasing a butterfly! At that moment I realized, I couldn't do it anymore! I couldn't follow her around everywhere, all the time! I couldn't see her all of the time! But God could! God's eyes are bigger and better than mine! He can see everything!

Jeremiah 29:11 is a verse that always remains close to my heart. God knows the plans that he has for me and Katie. He doesn't want to harm us or cause us any pain, and he wants to give us a hope and a future!

Trusting in these words has given me my life back! Though some days are harder than others, my peace and hope come from God.

Luke 15, 4-7 Suppose one of you has a hundred sheep & loses one of them. Does he not leave the ninety-nine in the open country & go after the lost sheep until he find it. [5] And when he find it, he joyfully puts it on his Shoulders [6] & goes home. Then he calls his friends & neighbors together & says "Rejoice with me" I have found my lost sheep. [7] I tell you that in the same way there will be more rejoicing in heaven over one sinner who repents than over ninety-nine rightous persons who do not need to repent.

Hi - I'm Dan DeRose the boys call me Big Papa. We're all sinners, Lost sheep open to Gods love

It's great to realize what a loving & forgiving God we have. Asking forgiveness & accepting it will give ya a changed heart & eternal Life. What a good God we have. They party in heaven when one of us is found.

Let Heaven Party
&
God Bless us All.

Personal reflections...

"For everything that was written in the past was written to teach us, so that through endurance and the encouragement of the Scriptures we might have hope." Romans 15:4

What a power__ful__ verse, especially during the times we live in!

As a Christian, we are not promised an easier life, but we are promised an A__bundan__t life. We are promised an abundance of peace, love, joy and hope. HOW ENCOURAGING! All we have to do is accept the invitation from our Heavenly Father to walk hand in hand with Him through A__LL__ of life's journey.

Remember, God is truth.

He cannot lie. Therefore, ALL of His Word is true. If He promises a life of abundance, even in a world that wants to rob us of all of that, then we can trust Him.

So, walk with our Father through His Word to find encouragement and hope. I promise you will never be disappointed. I have found all of God's promises to be true through every trial of my own life. God is my love, my joy, my peace, my encouragement and my hope!

Kim

Psalm 118: 1, 24 Give thanks to the Lord, for he is good; his love endures forever... This is the day the Lord has made; let us rejoice and be glad in it.

My name is Amanda, when I was young my mom would encourage my brothers and I to say this passage every morning. There were many days when I just didn't even want to get out of bed let alone face the day rejoicing. Reminding myself that the Lord is good and that he loves me always gives me hope to face the day. When I recite this passage in the morning, it helps me put the day in perspective. I start looking for nuggets that the Lord gives such as flowers, sunshine, fresh snow, kind words from someone, etc... This in turn reminds me to be a blessing in someone else's life. When you start recognizing all the good that God gives you on a daily basis your attitude starts looking up toward God instead of inward at personal problems.

I also like to recite this passage in the middle of a bad day. When I say it, I actually laugh at myself, for getting down about such a small issue. Because when I remember how big and great God is and how much he cares about me, I know he will get me through whatever trial I am facing. This passage has really helped keep a smile on my face and my face focused on God, the one who loves and cares for me every minute of every day!

Jesus said, "I am the vine, you are the branches; he who abides in Me and I in him will bear much fruit, for

 apart from Me you can do nothing."

John 15:5

Hi! My name is Trish and God has called me to be a writer. For weeks though, I have struggled with this assignment — to write to you!

I would start and stop in frustration, realizing that even though I was using God's word, something was not "quite right." Every attempt that I made ended in failure... and no one likes to fail, right? So even with my deadline in sight, rather than fail again, I gave up!

This is just what God wanted me to do. For from this experience, God showed me what He wanted ME to understand and share with you!

 Apart from Me, you can do
 NOTHING!

Have you ever picked up a pen and found that it wouldn't write? Most of us would take the pen, perhaps scribble a bit and then shake it up and down with the hope of encouraging the ink into the tip. I think that something similar happens in our lives too...

When God has a plan to use us for His purposes, and we resist that plan, He gets our attention by scribbling and shaking us too!

 How is the ink in your pen?

There have been times when God has asked me to do something and I respond by giving Him all sorts of excuses of why I can't . . . never realizing that THIS is His point :

I can't but He Can!

It took some Divine "shaking" in my life for me to realize that I must depend upon God for ALL things . . . apart from Him, I can do NOTHING!

I have discovered that all God wants me to do is BE the pen . . . HE IS THE INK!

What about you – are you trying to do things in your own power? Are you willing to be His instrument?

God often calls us to hard work; but God does not call us to work hard! He calls us to rest in His hand.

Hi, my name is Matt. Check out Ephesians 5: 3-5...

"But among you there must not even be a hint of sexual immorality, or of any kind of impurity, or of greed, because these are important for God's holy people. Nor should there be obscenity, foolish talk, or coarse joking, which are out of place, but rather thanksgiving. For of this you can be sure: No immoral, impure or greedy person - such a man is an idolater - has any inheritance in the kingdom of Christ and of God."

After reading this book, some of you may be interested in spending your life serving God; hopefully, a lot of you have already made that decision. Well, for just a moment I would like to share with you my heart and an example of how making that decision has improved my life.

When I was 17 years old I started dating this girl. She was kind, funny, beautiful and even had a relationship with God. What more could I have asked for? Things started off well and I was having the time of my life. However, as I began to rely on her, instead of God, to fulfill my needs, things went downhill. We began doing things that were sexually inappropriate and wrong to satisfy what we thought were our needs and desires. I knew that as a child of God (which is what God considers anyone who apologizes to him for what they've done wrong and asks him to take control of their life) what I was doing with my girlfriend went against my standards. But I didn't care, it felt right. As time went on, despite my ongoing relationship with my girlfriend, I felt alone, very alone. Not only that, but I felt unsatisfied, frustrated, angry, unloved, and like the life I created was falling apart, and it was out of my control. As a last resort I turned to God, pleading for help and telling him that I couldn't go on alone like this anymore. He replied simply this, "I love you, and I want to be with you more than you could ever want to be with me. Stop letting the mistakes of your past keep you from me. I love you." As I broke into tears I apologized for all I had done wrong. As I wondered what to do next he put the reference Ephesians 5:3-5 in my thoughts and wouldn't let me forget it. He used these verses to explain to me that if I really wanted all that he could offer me, I had to stop sinning with my girlfriend and break up with her. So I did. And although at first it was hard not having someone that close to hold and talk to, God fulfilled all of those needs for me. It is plain and simple; either you can rebel against God by doing the things listed in the verses and never have your needs and desires completely met, or you can trust God, listen to his rules, and accept the amazing life he is willing to give to you. I chose God, and God is the only reason I have had the strength to carry on. What will you choose today? God Bless

Matthew 25:40

"The King will reply, 'I
tell you the truth, whatever
you did for one of the
least of these brothers of
mine, you did for me.'"

My name is Anita, and I always
look forward to our family vacation
in Ocean City, NJ. For a few years,
my youngest daughter, Rachel, had
been asking me to buy her a hermit
crab from one of the shops on the
boardwalk. Next to snakes, hermit
crabs (yuk!) would be the "least"
desirable pets, in my opinion, so I
somehow avoided buying one for her-
until last year.

So, I bought a hermit crab! Rachel
was incredibly responsible and
affectionate with her new pet. She
named it, and treated it like a
queen (or King - who knows!) I was
impressed.

A couple weeks later, Rachel
went to camp. She said goodbye
and asked me to promise to care
for her crab, which made me
especially tender toward her.
When I went back to the house

and into my bedroom, I found the cage on my dresser. And beside the cage, lay a note - a love note from Rachel, sharing her affection for me and her gratitude that I would take care of her crab.

Wow! At that moment, my whole attitude changed toward the crab! I suddenly loved the crab and wanted to take the best care of it - not because it was a crab, but because it was Rachel's special pet. I love Rachel. And whatever and whoever Rachel loves, then I will love too.

And just as quickly as my attitude changed, my spiritual "light bulb" came on. I had just experienced what Jesus meant when He talked about the, "least of these brothers."

All week long, I loved and cared for that crab, and knew that I was really loving and caring for Rachel.

There are more analogies. Do you see them?
- the love note is like Gods WORD - Bible.
- the cage was in my room - God has put people in our care.

"For Me to live is Christ
to die is gain."

Phillipians 1:21

God had called my
wife and I to serve
Him from the beginning
of our marriage. We
were dedicated to
live and serve Him
as pastor + wife.

It was only a few
years after that we
were told that she
had only six weeks
to six months to live.
Her first words were
"I am ready to go"

Our trust in Christ remained firm. We continued to serve Him and she did not die of that type of cancer.

Some years later she got pancreatic cancer But we still served, and lived for Christ

In 2001, she met the Lord. a result of a third kind of cancer. My friend, she is not dead. But more alive than she was here.

It is worth living for Christ.

Hi,

My name is Linda and not so long ago, I heard a word that has really changed my life! That word is "perspective".

I have often heard the phrase, "Is the glass half full or half empty?" Now that is a picture of perspective.

It says in Phil 4:12, "I have learned the secret of being content in any and every situation". For me, that secret is perspective! Not my perspective, but God's perspective.

Let me give you some examples:

I can complain because my clothes fit too snuggly, but it really means I have enough to eat.

I can complain about the piles of laundry I have to do, but it really means I have a family to care for

My kids can complain that I'm strict and have too many rules and curfews but it really means that I love them enough to care.

So...
    I challenge you, to change your perspective. Look for the good in people, the blue in the sky, the hand of God, and the feet of Jesus. He'll never let you walk alone. Why?

    Because the glass really is half full, and God really does Love you!!

What do I think about this?

_____

_____

_____

_____

_____

_____

_____

_____

_____

_____

_____

_____

"I can do all Things Through Christ who strengthens me" Philippians 4:13

My name is Nancy Bergum. Last summer I wiped out water skiing and injured my shoulder. It was one of the most painful things I've ever experienced in my life. Over a period of a few months my everyday tasks became increasingly difficult and filled with pain. I had torn my rotator cuff tendon and developed a condition called "frozen shoulder". During the 5 months of physical therapy I cried out to God to heal my shoulder and take away the pain. There were so many things I could not do. I was beginning to loose hope, until one day, when I was reading Gods word. "I can do all things through Christ who strengthens me" was right in front of my eyes. This was the thread that kept me hanging on. These words helped me to keep my focus when all else seemed to be out of my control. 5 months of therapy completed and it was now time for surgery. Yikes!!! In the process, They damaged a nerve in my shoulder which has impaired my recovery. The pain I experienced before surgery seems pale in comparison to now. Things feel more out of control than ever before and there is more I cannot do. There are times when the mountain ahead of me seems impossible.

I can honestly say that the only thing that helps me keep my focus, to do when I cannot do, when things are out of my control, is that fact that "I can do all things through Christ who strengthens me." Without God's word, I would have been swallowed up by all the things I could not do and given up hope of recovery. I am still in therapy and the mountain is still in front of me, but everyday I keep climbin'. I have learned to hold on to the words, to hold on to God's love for me. This is what will give me strength when I am weak. Don't ever give up, no matter how bleak your circumstances may look because you can do all things through Christ who strengthens you! ☺

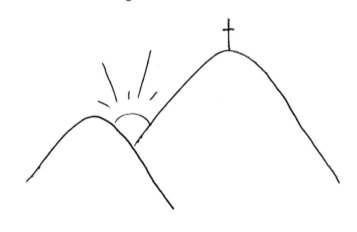

"Give yourselves to God...
Surrender your whole being to
Him to be used for righteous
purposes."

Romans 6:13

Hi, my name is Kristy and it
has taken me a long time to
understand what the word
"surrender" means. It is a
powerful word and action to
take but it is by no means
easy to do.

I have always been an
independent person and never
wanted to admit when I
couldn't do something on my
own. However, these past few
months God has shown me
that doing things on my own
or in my own strength is not
what God wants for me. It actually
caused me more stress and
took me further from His
plan for my life. Over the
past year I have surrendered
my future, my family life,
and also who God wants me
to spend the rest of my
life with. Not until then
did I start to see God's
power and faithfulness.

I knew that I had surrendered to God when I began to rely on Him to work things out instead of me trying to manipulate others, force my agenda, and control the situation. I let it all go and let Him work. And did He ever!! My future and purpose in life was more clear, relationships in my family are being healed, and God has blessed me with an amazing Godly man created for me. God wants our lives, all of it!! I promise that you will see God's hand in your life when you surrender it to Him.

He will be faithful!

What are you holding onto that is wearing you down?

What is keeping you from surrendering it to God right now?

Ephesians 3:14-19

"When I think of the wisdom and scope of God's plan, I fall to my knees and pray to the Father, the Creator of everything in heaven and earth. I pray that from his glorious, unlimited resources he will give you mighty inner strength through his Holy Spirit. And I pray that Christ will be more and more at home in your hearts as you trust in him. May your roots go down into the soil of God's marvellous love. And may you have the power to understand, as all God's people should, how wide, how long, how high and how deep his love really is. May you experience the love of Christ, though it is so great you will never fully understand it. Then you will be filled with the fullness of life and power that comes from God."

Hi, My name is Ben. I wanted to share these verses with you as there is a real hope in them however long you've been a Christian. God will give you strength to overcome any obstacle life may seem to throw at you. Better yet the more life seems to be against you, the more we all have to rely on the Holy Spirit to give us that strength. That strength is based solely in Gods love for us a love that is too wide to get around too long to run from, too high to outdo and too deep to out-love! There is no other love like it, it has no limits and living life in it makes life make sense!

For you are all sons of God through faith in Christ Jesus. For as many of you as were baptized into Christ have put on Christ. There is neither Jew nor Greek, there is neither slave nor free, there is neither male nor female; for you are all one in Christ Jesus.

Galatians 3:26-28

I'm Kate, a mom

I grew up at a time when everything was being questioned. The role of the government, how a man or woman should live, what was right or wrong, was all up for grabs. Lots of people and groups showed me models of how I should live as Jesus' follower. I know that I belong to Christ, and I am God's child because I believe in Him. I feel secure in this -- He loves me and accepts me where I am and as I am.

Notes...

Isaiah 41 v 13

For I am the Lord your God, who takes hold of your right hand and says to you, "Do not fear; I will help you".

Hi, I'm Abi.

People sometimes let us down, sometimes our friends and family the people who we trust the most let us down, at the times when we most need someone to hold us, hug us and encourage us we are alone.

God gave me this verse when

I was alone, insecure and unsure of my future. When the people I love are for some reason gone, He is holding my hand, He is standing right next to me because he loves me that much.

I often try to do things and I fail, when I do things by myself, things which look hard, which are impossible for me. He is helping me, going before me and through him you can do ANYTHING.

YOU ARE NOT ALONE

My thoughts...

*A new command I give you:

Love one another. As I have

loved you, so you must love

one another. *

John 13:34

Hello Hello! I'm Jennifer
Juliana ♡ I definately think
this verse is really sweet.

I love how Christ does not just tell us to love each other, but He Himself was a living example of that! Here's some random questions to ask yourself:

1. Do I truly put forth an effort to love people?

2. Does Christ want me to love the people who annoy me, or are just really hard to love?

3. How do I respond when people love me?

My feelings...

_____

_____

_____

_____

_____

_____

_____

_____

_____

_____

Do not let your hearts be troubled. Trust in God; trust also in me. In my Father's house are many rooms; if it were not so, I would have told you. I am going there to prepare a place for you. And if I go and prepare a place for you, I will come back and take you to be with me that you also may be where I am.

John 14:1-3 NIV

Did you ever wonder just how big heaven really is? Jesus tells us here in a straightforward way that there are many rooms with a place for each of us personally. But sometimes it's hard for me to have faith that my place as a forgiven child of God is really there. That's when I remember the first verse; Jesus' specific command not to be troubled but to trust in Him. That's what it boils down to. I believe He has a special place for me because I have full trust in His truth. God wants you to be with Him. Will you give Him your trust and let Him give you a room?

— Rachel

Personal reflections...

37 Jesus replied: "Love the Lord your God with all your heart and with all your soul and with all your mind. 38 This is the <u>first</u> and <u>greatest</u> commandment. 39 And the second is <u>like</u> it: 'Love your neighbor as yourself.'

Matthew 22: 37-39

My name is Adam Dole and I am an 18 yr. old Christian. This verse was Jesus's reply to what the greatest commandment God wants us to do is. They're pretty concise if you ask me. #1 commandment: <u>LOVE GOD</u>; #2 command: Love others (neighbors). It's important to note that Jesus said the second commandment is "like" the first. That's important to me because it's, in a nutshell, saying loving God goes hand in hand with loving people.

Here's some questions for thought.

1.) Can you do the first commandment without the second?

2.) Is it possible to not love someone you can see and love someone you can't?

Notes...

_____
_____
_____
_____
_____
_____
_____
_____
_____
_____
_____
_____
_____
_____
_____
_____
_____
_____

"And the God of grace, who called you to his eternal glory in Christ, after you have suffered a little while, will himself restore you and make you strong, firm, and steadfast."

1 Peter 5:10

~^~^~^~^~^~^~^~^~^~^~^~^~^~

Hey! I'm Bonnie and I really want to tell you how this verse helped get me through an extremely difficult time in my life.

I had been dating someone for four years and engaged to him for one of those years.

God chose to take the man I love away from me just two months ago. He did not die but the grief was and is very real. When the relationship ended, at times I felt that my life was also ending. I wanted to completely shut down.

During one of my many crying spells, I cried out to God in

pain asking for... anything!
I just needed something. I heard
him say to me " 1 Peter 5:" I thought
"yeah right - that is just me talking"
But I kept hearing it! So I figured
I had nothing to loose & turned
there, to the verse I shared! As soon
as I read it I cried - cried hard -
harder than I had been crying. God
had **heard** me! He had **seen** me! He
knew my pain & came to me i_n_ that
pain. He met me where I was at.
when I'm in pain nothing anyone
says helps - but God is not like
other people! He knows exactly
where I'm at (where you'_re_ at!) and
what I need to hear & he meets me
there.
My life has been changing a lot
and changing with it has been
extremly difficult but ya know
what?

God is restoring me like he
promised and he says he'll
only let me "suffer a little
while."

JOHN 8:34-36

Jesus replied, "I assure you that everyone who sins is a slave to sin. A slave is not a permanent member of the family, but a son is part of the family forever. So if the Son sets you free, you will indeed be free."

Hi! My name's Jewel and here's a little something just for you!

WHEN I READ THIS I KNOW THAT:

* EVERYONE is guilty of sin!

* If you are allowing sin to take over your life, you cannot be a member of God's family.

* If you ask Jesus to free you from your sins you will be free from them FOREVER!

NOW, ASK YOURSELF:

★ Have I let sin take over my life?

★ Do I want to be freed from my sin + the guilt that comes with it?

★ Do I want to spend forever in hell, or live forever in heaven as a part of God's family?

Personal reflections...

_____
_____
_____
_____
_____
_____
_____
_____
_____
_____
_____
_____
_____
_____
_____
_____

MATTHEW 6:25-27

25 So I tell you, dont worry about the food or drink you need to live, or about the clothes you need for your body. Life is more than food, & the body is more than clothes. **26** Look at the birds in the air. They don't plant or harvest or store food in barns, but your heavenly father feeds them. And you know that you are worth much more than birds. **27** You cannot add any time to your life by worrying about it.

Hi my name is James and I'm from the southwest of England. I go to the sort of school that is <u>really</u> hyped up about how you do in exams.

This year I did my G.C.S.E's and during that time I started to get worried, like everyone else about how I'd do. What if I failed? What would I do? But then I was sent this verse by a family friend. It was really helpful. Because although we might not be homeless without food or clothing, the verse can apply to alot. Especially skool, college and uni. What God's saying here is that you're more important than the birds and do they worry?

NO! So why do you? God's here to help us, just ask and he's here.

"U cn not + time 2 ur life by worryin about it!"

What do I think about this?

_____

_____

_____

_____

_____

_____

_____

_____

_____

_____

_____

_____

_____

_____

_____

_____

_____

_____

Matthew 16:24-27

(24) Then Jesus said to his disciples "If anyone would come after me he must deny himself take up his cross and follow me.

(25) For whoever wants to save his life will lose it, but whoever looses his life for me will find it.

(26) What good will it be for a man if he gains the whole world yet forfeits his soul.

(27) For the son of Man is going to come in his Father's glory with his angels, and then he will reward each person according to what he has done.

Hey, I'm MANDY... this is some stuff I learned from the verses.

(24) If we want the best thing we could ever have (which is Jesus) we must give up our selfish desires an do what he wants us to do.

(25) If you want control, & you try to keep control, you will lose it. You should trust God to be in control & if you do he will give you peace of Mind.

(26) Things of the world are unimportant & often times we think we are getting "Things" when really its the world taking from us, sucking our soul dry.

(27) God loves us and appreciates us and if we love him and appreciate Him we will want to do good things for us, just like he wants to do good things for us.

Personal reflections...

2 Samuel 22 v 17-20

He reached down from heaven & rescued me; he drew me from my powerful enemies, from those who hated me & were too strong for me. They attacked me at a moment when I was weakest, but the Lord upheld me. He led me to a place of safety; he rescued me because he delights in me.

I'm Briony and this verse means so much to me because I found at a time when I was so depressed & low that i'd tried to commit suicide! This verse was a total God send! He lifted my self esteem and bought home the fact that God rescues & delivers us when we need him. When we fight battles, he fights with us and sees that justice is done.

This verse also shows how much God loves us all.

Take pride in being his child for he is always with you!

Notes...

_____
_____
_____
_____
_____
_____
_____
_____
_____
_____
_____
_____
_____
_____
_____
_____
_____
_____

You open your hand, and satisfy the _desires_ of every living thing. The Lord is righteous in all His ways, and loving toward all He has made. The Lord is near to all who call on Him, to all who call on Him in truth. He fulfills the _desires_ of those who fear Him, He hears their cry and saves them.

PSALM 145:16-19

Hi,

My name is Maria, and I want to share something that totally changed my life and view of God. Although I always knew that He loved me and wants what's best for me, I never thought that my desires and His desires could be the same. You see, my heart desperately desires to have a successful music ministry. The greatest thing I could ever picture in my life, is to travel with my "musician husband" (whom I don't have yet), be signed to a great Christian record label, and bring hope to many who are hurting through music! This dream of mine, however, seems way too unrealistic and unobtainable, so for a long time, I never prayed for it or bothered to ask God if it would ever be an option for me. I always thought that God would give me a nice, ordinary, boring life. Well, I reached a very low point in my life, where in true despair, I just longed so deeply for this impossible goal. I opened up the Bible

To the back of Psalms, and was blown away at how directly God chose to address this pressing issue that was weighing me down tremendously, & taking away the joy out of everything I was doing in my life. And as I read, the word "desires" almost screamed out at me as in neon flashing lights. I kept reading, and just a few lines later, I saw that word again. Now it really got my attention. I decided to go back and read the whole thing over again and let it sink in. These verses were telling me that God wants to satisfy the desires of every living thing. That would include me! What really surprised me, was that it wasn't referring to God meeting our needs, which I almost expect, but my desires? He actually wants to give me what I desire, and not just what I need? It also says that the Lord is loving toward all He has made and that He is near to all who call on Him in truth, & if we look up to Him and trust Him, once again, it says that He will fulfil our desires. It also says that He hears our cries. That's exactly where I was. I was crying because I had a desire that I never thought God would want to fulfil. I never actually thought He cared about that stuff. After all, He's got wars to settle, hungry to feed. Why would He care about my desires? This whole passage has changed my life. I now see God as being on my side & cheering for me and for what I desire. He wants to make me happy 'cause the Bible says He loves me. Well, that desire is not fulfilled yet, but I'm surely on my way. And the best part of all, is... now I trust Him. I know He's on my side!

"Then Jesus said, "Come to me, all of you who are weary and carry heavy burdens, and I will give you rest.

Take my yoke upon you and let me teach you because I am humble and gentle, and you will find rest for your souls.

For my yoke fits perfectly, and the burden I give you is light."
(Matt. 11:28-30 N.L.T.)

Hi! My name is Juanita and my question is this: "Have you ever felt weary - right down to your very soul?" And "Did you know you can really find rest for your soul?" Let me explain:

As a 13 year old girl, I couldn't believe how tired I was of trying to please my parents, my teachers and all the adults around me. Even the kids wanted me to be just like them. Everybody's expectations were different. I never felt I had the freedom to "just be me." And worse yet - I didn't even know who I was - or how to find out! So I just kept thinking if I pleased all the people I was involved with, the day HAD to come when I'd feel "accepted" - and then the pressure would be off!

Imagine my shock that Sunday in church when I heard the minister read to ME (my racing heart told me so)... Jesus' invitation and promise of rest for my soul. Oh how I wanted that kind of rest!

But I was so afraid I'd have to miss out on a lot of fun things if I let Jesus teach me how to live a God-pleasing life.

So I struggled another 27 years - when I was really burned out from trying to please a husband, 3 kids, a boss, my parents, and everybody else I came in contact with.

But when I heard another minister in a _different_ church and denomination read the _same verse_ to me from the pulpit (my heart did that racing thing again)... I said "YES" to Jesus' invitation right then and there!

I _knew_ I couldn't possibly find true rest for my soul any other place or way (... fun or not...). I had tried!

And now at age 66, I can truthfully say it was the BEST decision I ever made! For the past 26 years, Jesus/Holy Spirit has been my constant companion, comforter, teacher, friend — and SO much more!

NOW my question is this: "Why don't you accept Jesus' invitation (either for the first time — or in a closer way) for the God-rest that only HE can give?"

"For all who enter into God's rest will find rest from their labors, just as God rested, after creating the world."
(Heb. 4:10 N.L.T.)

The Bible also says:
"Anyone who believes in Him will not be disappointed."
(Ro. 10:11 N.L.T.)

"Anyone who calls on the name of the Lord will be saved."
(Ro. 10:13 N.L.T.)

-Why not call today?
-He's _expecting_ your call!

The Crucifixion of Jesus Christ

The Thorn Crown of the King

So Pilate took Jesus and had him whipped. The soldiers, having braided a crown from thorns, set it on his head, threw a purple robe over him, and approached him with, "Hail, King of the Jews!" Then they greeted him with slaps in the face.

Pilate went back out again and said to them, "I present him to you, but I want you to know that I do not find him guilty of any crime." Just then Jesus came out wearing the thorn crown and purple robe. Pilate announced, "Here he is the Man."

When the high priests and police saw him, they shouted in a frenzy, "Crucify! Crucify!"

Pilate told them, "You take him. You crucify him. I find nothing wrong with him."

The Jews answered, "We have a law, and by that law he must die because he claimed to be the Son of God."

Pilate caved into their demand. He turned him over to be crucified. They took Jesus away.

The Crucifixion

Carrying his cross, Jesus went out to the place called Skull Hill (the name is Golgotha), where they crucified him, and with him two others, one on each side, Jesus in the middle.

When they crucified him, the Roman soldiers took his clothes and divided them up four ways, to each soldier a fourth. But his robe was seamless, a single piece of weaving, so they said to each other, "Let's not tear it up. Let's throw dice to see who gets it."

This confirmed the Scripture that siad, "They divided up my clothes among them and threw dice for my coat." (The soldiers validated the Scriptures!)

Jesus, then said, "I'm thirsty."

A jug of sour wine was standing by. Someone put a sponge soaked with the wine on a jhavelin and lifted it to his mouth. After he took the wine, Jesus said, "It's done...complete." Bowing his head, he offered up his spirit.

One of the soldiers stabbed him in the side with his spear. Blood and water gushed out. The eyewitness to these things has presented an accurate report. He saw it himself and is telling the truth so that you, also, will believe.

Resurrection

Early in the morning on the first day of the week, while it was still dark, Mary Magdalene came to the tomb and saw that the stone was moved away from the entrance. She ran at once to Simon Peter and the other disciple, the one Jesus loved, breathlessly panting, "They took the Master from the tomb.

We don't know where they've put him."

Peter and the other disciple left immediately for the tomb. They ran, neck and neck. The other disciple got to the tomb first, outrunning Peter. Stooping to look in, he saw the pieces of linen cloth lying there, but he didn't go in.

The disciples then went back home.

But Mary stood outside the tomb weeping. As she wept, she knelt to look into the tomb and saw two angels sitting there, dressed in white, one at the head, the other at the foot of where Jesus' body had been laid.

They said to her, "Woman, why do you weep?"

"They took my Master," she said, "and I don't know where they put him." After she said this, she turned away and saw Jesus standing there. But she didn't recognize him.

Jesus spoke to her, "Woman, why do you weep? Who are you looking for?"

She, thinking he was the gardener, said, "Mister, if you took him, tell me where you put him so I can care for him."

Jesus said, "Mary."

Turning to face him, she said in Hebrew, "Rabboni!" meaning "Teacher!"

Jesus said, "Don't cling to me, for I have not yet ascended to the Father. Go to my brothers and tell them, "I ascend to my Father and your Father, my God and your God."

Mary Magdelene went, telling the news to the disciples: "I saw the Master!" and she told them everything he said to her.

To Believe

Later on that day, the disciples had gathered together, but, fearful of the Jews, had locked all the doors in the house. Jesus entered, stood among them, and said, "Peace to you."

Then he showed them his hands and side. The disciples, seeing the Master with their own eyes, were exuberant.

Jesus repeated his greeting: "Peace to you. Just as the Father sent me, I send you." Then he took a deep breath and said, "If you forgive someone's sins, they're gone for good. If you don't forgive sins, what are you going to do with them?"

These are written down so you will believe that Jesus is the Messiah, the Son of God, and in the act of believing, have real and eternal life in the way he personally revealed it.

What do I do now?

You may now sense that something is missing from your life. You're feeling an emptiness only God can fill and all you have to do is ask Him! I know it sounds strange, talking to someone you can't see or touch, but it's not hard. And you can't mess up! Just speak to God openly and honestly from your heart. Ask Him to forgive you for all the ways you have sinned against Him by violating His laws and then confess your belief, without reservation, that Christ died on the cross to pay the penalty for your sins and that God raised Him from the dead. With this, God will forgive you for your sins and fill that emptiness with His Spirit. You are now "born again" as Jesus said in the Bible, in the book of John, chapter 3 and verse 7.

As a new follower of Jesus Christ, read the Bible daily. It's the best way to grow this new relationship. We suggest you start with the Book of John.

Most importantly, don't ever be afraid to share your weakness with God. He will give you the strength you need to turn away from sinful things. Plus, there are other followers of Christ who can come along side of you and support you. Find someone who has a strong relationship with Christ and share your victories and mistakes with him or her. They can encourage you and lighten the burden of making those mistakes.

God is offering unconditional love; all He wants is for you to truly love Him back. So take the step now and place every part of your life in His hands. If you can do that, He'll do the rest.

"So here's what I want you to do, God helping you: Take your everyday, ordinary life - your sleeping, eating, going to work and walking around life - and place it before God as an offering. Embracing what God does for you is the best thing you can do for him. So don't become so well adjusted to your culture that you fit in without even thinking. Instead, fix your attention on God. You'll be changed from the inside out. Readily recognize what God wants from you, and quickly respond to it, unlike the culture around you, always dragging you down to it's level of immaturity."

God brings out the
best in you

Romans 12:1-2, The Message

Notes

Notes

Notes

Notes

We believe the Bible, both Old and
New Testaments, to be the perfect and
innerrant Word of God. We encourage you
to secure the complete Bible soon for a deep
and more complete insight into
God's truth.

The Handwritten Bible has been comprised
of entries from people of many denominations
and church affiliations.

Many versions of the Bible were used including:
King James, New International, The Message,
New Analytical, New Living Translation,
Today's English and New American Standard.